The LIGHT SHINES In The DARKNESS

GEORGIANNA SUMMERS

A CHRISTMAS EVE
CANDLELIGHT SERVICE AND STORY

C.S.S. Publishing Co., Inc.

Lima, Ohio

THE LIGHT SHINES IN THE DARKNESS

7874 / ISBN 0-89536-888-9

PRINTED IN U.S.A.

Introduction

This service can be adapted in a variety of ways to meet the needs of individual congregations. Those churches who traditionally have communion on Christmas Eve will find it leads naturally into communion. However, it can be done just as effectively without communion. The music can be done solely by the congregation or can be varied with soloists and/or choir. Only traditional carols are suggested, but other appropriate music can be substituted, especially if a soloist or choir is used. The service can be dramatized with Mary, Joseph, shepherds, wisemen, etc. in tableaux at appropriate times, but it is not necessary.

The Christ candle should be a single white candle on the altar, unlit when the service begins. If four Advent candles have been used during the Sundays of Advent, they should also be unlit until the designated time in the service. The church may be decorated with candlelabra, candles in the windows, etc., but they too should be unlit until the appropriate time. As people arrive, ushers should give each person over ten years of age a small candle with a cardboard drip catcher, to be used at the end of the service.

The opening part of the service can include a call to worship, opening hymn, litany, prayer or whatever the minister desires. Any announcements or directions for the congregation should be given before the narration begins.

Part 1
The Service

Reader 1: (Can be the minister)
The people who walked in darkness — (Pause)
They knew darkness,
Those who lived in Palestine
Two thousand years ago.
They knew the darkness of oppression,
Of hatred and prejudice.
They lived in the shadow of hunger and disease
Cowered in the dim recesses of fear,
And cried out from the black depths of despair.
There were some who said,

Reader 2: (Male)
"Wait! Your God will come to save you.
He will come as a mighty warrior
To throw off the yoke of oppression
And bring in the Day of the Lord."

Reader 1: But others remembered what Isaiah had said:

Reader 2: "The people who walked in darkness
Have seen a great light.
They that dwell in the land of the shadow of
death
Upon them has the light shined.
For unto us a child is born,
Unto us a son is given:
And the government shall be upon his shoulder,
And his name shall be called Wonderful
Counselor,
Mighty God, Everlasting Father,
the Prince of Peace."

Congregational Hymn "O Come, O Come, Emmanuel"
(During the singing of this hymn four Advent
candles may be lit.)

Reader 1: Then in the days of Herod, the
king of Judea,
Elizabeth, the wife of Zechariah a priest,
Conceived a child in her old age.
In her sixth month she was visited by her
cousin, Mary.
But let Elizabeth speak.

Reader 3: (Female)
I remember that visit well.
When my cousin Mary entered our house and
greeted me,
The babe leaped in my womb for joy,
And I cried out in a loud voice,
"Blessed are you among women."
And she told me of the angel Gabriel's visit
And his very same words to her.
She shared how frightened and troubled she was
At his greeting, and how he said,
"Fear not, Mary, for you have found favor with
God.
And behold you shall conceive in your womb
And bring forth a son,
And shall call his name Jesus."
And Mary said:

Reader 4: (Female — read, or else sung as a solo; or,
chanted by a choir)
"My soul magnifies the Lord,
And my spirit rejoices in God my Savior,
For he has regarded the low estate of his
handmaiden.
For behold, henceforth all generations will call
me blessed;
For he who is mighty has done great things
for me,
And holy is his name.
And his mercy is on those who fear him
From generation to generation.
He has shown strength with his arm,
He has scattered the proud in the imagination of
their hearts. He has put down the mighty from
their thrones,

And exalted those of low degree;
He has filled the hungry with good things,
And the rich he has sent empty away.
He has helped his servant Israel,
In remembrance of his mercy,
As he spoke to our fathers,
To Abraham and to his posterity forever."

Reader 3: And Mary stayed with me about three months
And returned to her own house in Nazareth.

Reader 1: And it came to pass in those days
That there went out a decree from
Caesar Augustus
That all the world should be taxed.
And all went to be taxed,
Everyone into his own city.

Reader 2: And I, Joseph, also went up from Galilee,
Out of the city of Nazareth into Judea
Unto the city of David,
which is called Bethlehem,
Because I was of the house and lineage
of David.
And I brought with me my betrothed, Mary,
Who was close to her time of childbirth.

Reader 4: How well I remember the journey.
It was long and slow
Because I could not travel far without resting.
I was anxious because I was afraid the
baby would come
Before we found shelter.
And I remember it was with great relief
That we finally came to Bethlehem.
Joseph took us straight to the inn,
But the private rooms were taken,
And the courtyard was crowded with travelers
Who, like us, had come to register for the
census.
The baby had started to come,
And there was no place of privacy for us there.
The innkeeper took us to a cave behind the inn
Where the animals were sheltered.

It was quiet and private
And warmed by the bodies of the animals.
And there it was that he was born — my Jesus.
And I wrapped him in swaddling clothes
And laid him in a manger.

(At this point the Christ candle should be lit and the four Advent candles extinguished.)

Congregational Hymn "Away In A Manger"

An appropriate solo or choir anthem can be substituted.)

Reader 1: And there were in the same country
Shepherds abiding in the field,
Keeping watch over their flock by night.

Reader 2: We were asleep — most of us.
I remember it was my turn to stand watch,
And I too was half asleep
Because the night was so quiet and undisturbed
Even by the sound of wolf or jackal.
Suddenly the sky began to glow with an
unearthly light.
I cried out in fear to my companions,
"Wake up! The sky is on fire !"
Then it was that we saw the angel
And realized that the light was
The glory of the Lord shining 'round about us.
We were afraid, but the angel said,

Reader 1: "Fear not, for behold I bring you
Good tidings of great joy
Which shall be to all people.
For unto you is born this day
In the city of David
A savior which is Christ the Lord.
And this shall be a sign unto you:
You shall find the babe wrapped in swaddling
clothes,
Lying in a manger."

Reader 2:   And suddenly there was with the angel
A multitude of the heavenly host,
Praising God and saying:
"Glory to God in the highest
And on earth peace, good will toward men."
Then the angels went away,
And we said to each other,
"Let us go to Bethlehem
And see this thing which is come to pass
Which the Lord had made known to us."
So we came as quickly as possible
And found Mary and Joseph,
And the babe lying in a manger.

Congregational Hymn "The First Noel" *Verses 1 and 2*
(An appropriate solo or choir anthem can be substituted.)

Reader 1:   And later there came wisemen
From the east to Jerusalem,
Saying, "Where is he that is born
King of the Jews?
For we have seen his star in the east
And are come to worship him."

Reader 2:   We came to Herod because we assumed
A king would be born in a palace.
But I remember how troubled
Herod was by our questions.
He called his chief priests and scribes together
Who said we should search in Bethlehem.
Herod asked us to bring him word
When we found the babe
So that he too could come and worship him.
So once again we followed the star
Until it came and stood over where the
young child was.
We fell down and worshiped him
And presented him with our gifts —
Gold, frankincense, and myrrh.
But we did not return to Herod,

For God warned us in a dream that we
should not.
So we returned to our own country another way.

Congregational Hymn *"We Three Kings"* or
"What Child Is This? or
"As With Gladness Men of Old"

Offering
Reader 1: After the wise men had left, an angel of
the Lord
Appeared in a dream to Joseph and said,
"Herod will be looking for the child in order
to kill him.
So get up, take the child and his mother and
escape to Egypt,
And stay there until I tell you to leave."
Joseph got up, took the child and his
mother,
And left during the night for Egypt.

Reader 2: When Herod realized that the visitors from the East
Had tricked him, he was furious.
He gave orders to kill all the boys in Bethlehem
And its neighborhood who were two years old
and younger . . .
In this way what the prophet Jeremiah had said
came true:
"A sound is heard in Ramah,
The sound of bitter weeping.
Rachel is crying for her children;
she refuses to be comforted,
for they are dead."

Reader 1: After Herod died, an angel of the Lord
Appeared in a dream to Joseph in Egypt and
said,
"Get up, take the child and his mother,
And go back to the land of Israel,
Because those who tried to kill the child are
dead."

Reader 2: So Mary and Joseph returned to Galilee
To their own city, Nazareth.

And the child grew and became strong in spirit,
Filled with wisdom, and the grace of God was
upon him.

"Where is Our Lord?" A Story sermon for Christmas

Reader 2: Then in the fifteenth year of the
reign of Tiberius Caesar
The word of God came to John,
The son of Zechariah and Elizabeth,
And he went into all the region about
the Jordan,
Preaching a baptism of repentance
For the forgiveness of sins.
Then Jesus came from Galilee to the Jordan
To be baptized by John.

Reader 1: That's where some of us first met him.
We were John's disciples,
But John pointed him out and said,
"Behold the Lamb of God."
And we followed him.

Reader 2: He taught us many things —
About life, about truth,
About the way to find God.
"I am the way, the truth, and the life," he said.
I remember when he said this.
It was at that last meal together
Where he broke the bread and poured the wine
As a symbol of his body and blood given for us.
He asked us to continue this celebration
After he was gone — in remembrance of him.

Reader 3: There was so much to remember —
How he called us from our daily tasks to
follow him.
How he fed the hungry and healed the sick.
How he accepted all kinds of people —
The outcast, the poor, people of other races,
Women — even the hated Romans.

Reader 4: And I remember what he taught
In words as well as deeds.
"You are the light of the world —

The kingdom of heaven is within you —
If you have known me, you have known my
Father also."

Reader 1: And finally I remember what he told us to do —
"Seek first the kingdom of God.
Love your neighbor as yourself.
Love your enemy.
Be a servant.
Let your light so shine
That others will see your good works
And glorify your Father in heaven.
Do this — in remembrance of me."

Communion Hymn, Solo, or Anthem

(Suggested solo or anthem: "In Remembrance of Me" from
Celebrate Life by Buryl Red; Broadman Press, Nashville,
Tennessee; Code 4565-35)

(At this point communion may be served, if desired.)

Minister: And he who came into the world
As a babe in Bethlehem
Was the Word of God made flesh
That dwelt among us, full of grace and truth.
(House lights begin to go out.)
In him was life; and that life was the light of
the world.
That light shines in the darkness still,
And the darkness has not overcome it.
(Long Pause)
(All lights out except the Christ candle. Let the
congregation experience the single light shining
in the darkness for a moment of silence.)
We too who are his followers
Are the light of the world.

(At this point two candle lighters should come to the altar, light their tapers from the Christ candle, and begin spreading the light. They first light candlelabra or other candles around the sanctuary. Then they go down the aisles and light the candles of the end persons in each pew. They in turn light the candle of the person next to them and so on down the pews until everyone over ten years of age is holding a lighted candle. While this is being done the minister reads the following Scripture.)

This then is the message which we heard of him
And declare unto you —
That God is light, and in God is no darkness
at all.
If we walk in the light, as God is in the light,
We have fellowship one with another.

Those who love abide in the light,
But those who hate abide in darkness.
Therefore, beloved, let us love one another,
Not in word, neither in tongue,
But in deed and in truth.
For love is of God,
And everyone who loves is born of God and
knows God.

Herein is love, not that we loved God
But that God loved us
And sent His son to die on a cross.
Beloved, if God so loved us,
We ought also to love one another.
Therefore let us love one another.
And let our light shine.

Congregational Hymns "O Little Town of Bethlehem"
"Silent Night"
(Can be started while candles are still being lit.)

Benediction: Go now into the world
And light it with the love of God.
Feed the hungry.
Heal the sick.
Welcome the stranger.
Visit the lonely.

Make peace among the nations.
In remembrance of the babe of Bethlehem
Who became the light of the world.

Amen

(Candles are extinguished)

14

Part 2
Where Is Our Lord?
(A Story Sermon for Christmas Eve)

He was twelve years old although he was so small he could have passed for eight. His black hair and brown, paper-thin flesh stretched tautly across his small frame stood out in sharp contrast against the white sheets of the hospital bed. The young church worker sat quietly by his bed, holding his hand. As she studied his emaciated face, he slowly opened his eyes. There was bewilderment in them at first, then fear, the look of a hunted animal. She smiled kindly. Then he spoke in a hoarse whisper.

"Where — where am I?"

"You are in a hospital in Arizona in the United States," she answered him in Spanish. "We found you on the desert."

He struggled to sit up. "Mi madre?" he croaked hoarsely.

"We found her too. She" . . . She hesitated uncertainly. "We . . . we're taking care of her and the others we found. You must rest now." He relaxed and fell back on the bed.

"Tell me, what is your name?" she asked.

"Jesus," [pronounced Hay-soos throughout the story]

"That's a fine name," she said. "The best. And you are going to be fine too. You are safe now, Jesus. We are giving you food and liquids through this tube in your arm. Soon you will be strong enough to eat solid food. Do you understand?"

He nodded his head slightly. Then he closed his eyes. He wasn't sure he understood, although she did speak his language. It felt so good here. It was pleasantly cool. He had been so very hot in the day and so very cold at night. The bed was soft and smooth. The last he could remember was lying on the parched, hard ground, prickly weeds scratching his face, sand in his mouth. And his mother's hand on top of his. Where was his mother? Someone was patting his hand. Perhaps that was his mother. He slept.

When he awoke again, it was to bright sunlight. It was noisy with the bustle of activity around him. A woman's voice said loudly, "Well now, look who's awake," but he couldn't understand what she was saying. She put a smooth stick in his mouth and held his wrist, all the time talking in a strange language.

Then another lady came through the door carrying a tray of food. They propped him up in bed and fed him. It tasted good. And there was water to drink, lots of it. But he was worried. Where was his mother? "Mi madre," he said again and again, but they didn't seem to understand. Their voices were kind, and the first lady gave him a hug and held him against her for a long time. When she let him go, he noticed there were tears in her eyes. Then she laid him back in the bed and tucked him under the sheets before she left him.

He closed his eyes, and he remembered. He and his mother, his younger brothers and sisters, his Uncle Juan and Aunt Lupe, his cousins, other people from his country — all of them were walking across the desert.

Reader 2: "Joseph got up, took the child and his mother, and left during the night for Egypt."

(*Storyteller continues*) Everything was so dry and brown, not at all like his country where there were trees and flowers and water. El Salvador — how he missed it. He wanted to go back, but he couldn't. It wasn't safe. They had to escape.

Reader 2: "Herod will be looking for the child in order to kill him. So get up, take the child and his mother and escape to Egypt, and stay there until I tell you to leave."

(*Storyteller continues*) Uncle Juan paid a man to help them cross the border into the United States. He had not liked the man, but Uncle Juan said they had to trust him. When they crossed the border into the United States, they would be safe, Uncle Juan had said. But the man left them in the middle of the night while they were sleeping, and they were on their own. As he remembered, he began to cry. Then he felt a hand on his.

"Jesus," a woman's voice said. His mother! He opened his eyes.

It was not his mother. It was the young woman who spoke his language. "Mi madre?" he asked, sobbing.

"You must not worry about your mother, Jesus," the lady said. "She would want you to get strong and well." She held his hand and let him cry. After a while she said gently, "I think it would help, Jesus, if you could tell me what happened on the desert before we found you. Can you do that?"

He nodded. Then he told her how he and his family and other Salvadorans had paid the man to help them across the border, how they had wandered, not knowing where to go. He paused. It was hard to talk about what happened after that. He didn't want to remember.

Reader 2: "A sound is heard in Ramah, the sound of
bitter weeping.
Rachel is crying for her children;
She refuses to be comforted, for they are dead."

"Some of your family died, didn't they, Jesus?" she asked softly.
"Yes," he sobbed. "My little brothers and sisters, Aunt Lupe, my two cousins, then Uncle Juan. Only my mother and me left in my family. I fell down. I couldn't go any farther."
"I know. A farmer found you and the others who were still alive. He brought you here. You are safe now. We will take care of you."
"Who are you?" he asked. "What is your name?"
"My name is Margaret. I work for a church."
"The Catholic Church?"
"No, my church happens to be the Presbyterian, but we are all part of the Christian Church — Catholics, Methodists, Presbyterians, Lutherans, Quakers. We are all working together. Now, Jesus, I think it is time for you to rest."
"Will you come again?"
"Yes — every day. And I will bring a priest with me next time, a priest who speaks Spanish. Would you like that?"
"Yes," he said as his eyes closed, "and please — bring me my mother."
Jesus was dreaming now. He was in Salvador with his family. People had come to his home for Bible study and discussion. He was just a little boy and couldn't understand much, but he heard them talk about Christ and how he helped the poor. The priest said they must all work together to help the poor. He heard words like "justice" and "freedom."
Then in his dream he was with hundreds of other people, and Bishop Romero was speaking to them. The bishop was saying, "We suffer with those who have disappeared, those who have had to flee their homes . . . and those who have been tortured." People were crying. Then they were all marching and singing, "But where, where, where is our Lord? He is with the humble and the persecuted." It was a good dream.

Suddenly his dream changed to a nightmare. People were scream-ing. Soldiers with guns were shooting at them. The bishop was celebrating mass in the chapel. They were shooting the bishop. Jesus was screaming. Then a man's voice called his name.

"Jesus, Jesus, wake up. It's all right."

He opened his eyes. There was his priest. No, it was a different priest, but he was speaking in Spanish. "I am Father Thomas," he said. "Senorita Margaret told me about you. You must have been hav-ing a bad dream."

Jesus nodded. He was still frightened, his eyes darting around the room looking for the soldiers with guns.

Father Thomas said, "Tell me about your dream." So Jesus told him. When he had finished, the priest said, "You have seen too many cruel things, Jesus. Tell me, did the soldiers harm your family?"

Jesus' eyes filled with tears. "Yes, they shot my father. Then they took my Uncle Manuel away, and we never heard from him again. Next they came for my cousin Jose and put him in the army. He had to learn to kill his fellow Salvadorans — people like us. There was so much killing, even little babies."

Reader 2: **"When Herod realized that the visitors from the East had tricked him, he was furious. He gave orders to kill all the boys in Bethlehem and its neighborhood who where two years old and younger."**

(Storyteller continues) "Is that why your family came to the United States?" the priest asked.

"Yes. My mother was afraid they would take me for the army like they did Jose. Uncle Juan was afraid they would come for him in the middle of the night like they did for Uncle Manuel. We were all afraid for the little ones. But now they are all dead anyway — even my mother. She is dead too, isn't she?"

The priest reached over and took his hand. "I'm afraid so, Jesus. We didn't want to tell you until you were stronger." They sat in silence for a long time, the boy crying softly.

Finally Jesus said, "What will I do now, Father? Where will I go? Will they send me back?"

"No, Jesus, you will stay here. When you are strong enough to leave the hospital, we will find a home for you with a good family."

"Maybe I could stay with Senorita Margaret."

She would like that, but I don't think it's possible right now. She has — she has some business with the government that she has to take care of.

"Is she in trouble with the government ?"

"Well . . . in a way . . . yes."

"Because of me?"

"No, Jesus, not because of you. She is in trouble because she is a Christian."

"Then your government must be like mine. That is why we were in trouble. I thought things were different in the United States."

"They are, Jesus. Don't worry. She will not be killed or tortured, and she sends you her love. She will come to see you again soon. In the meantime we want you to eat well and get lots of rest. Would you like to learn English?"

Jesus nodded.

"Good. Then we will send you a teacher. Now I must leave you for a while. Here is a rosary to help comfort you and a Spanish Bible."

The next day another lady came to see him. She was warm and friendly, and she had a boy with her about his age. She spoke in Spanish. "My name is Senora Ortiz, Jesus, and this is my son Paul. We are going to teach you English. The doctor says you are strong enough now to get up and walk around; so we have brought you a present."

Paul handed him a big box. It was full of clothes. As he took them out. Senora Ortiz smiled and said, "Your English lesson begins right now. Repeat after me — pants, shirt, socks."

Then Paul went out into the hall and came back in with a thick wooden club. He grinned as he handed it to Jesus. "Baseball bat," he said.

"This is for you to have fun with when your are stronger," Senora Ortiz explained. "Paul will teach you how to play."

A few days later as he was walking down the hall to visit his fellow Salvadorans who were still in the hospital, Jesus heard a familiar voice calling to him. He turned quickly.

Senorita Margaret!" He was overjoyed. "I was so afraid they had taken you away to prison."

"No, Jesus. I have a good lawyer; so do not worry. We will trust in God. Come now, let's go back to your room. I have good news for you."

"What is it?" he asked as they reached his room.

"The doctor says you are strong enough to leave the hospital, and the Ortiz family say they would like to have you live with them. Would you like that?"

"Yes, very much. Paul is going to teach me to play baseball. But won't I ever see you again?"

"Of course you will. We are all a family now — you, the Ortizes, Father Thomas, your fellow Salvadorans, the families who are helping them. We will meet together each week."

"And practice our English?"

She laughed. "Right. And we will study the Bible as you did in your village. We will have a Base Christian Community right here."

"And the soldiers will not come?"

She hesitated just a second. "No, Jesus. You will be safe."

"Senorita?"

"Yes, Jesus?"

"Why do you do this for us — feed us, clothe us, take us in your homes, perhaps even go to prison for us? We are only poor peasants from a foreign land."

She was thoughtful for a moment. "Why? I think the best answer is in the Bible. Here, let me read it to you." She reached over to his bedside table and picked up the Spanish Bible Father Thomas had brought him. "It's in Matthew 25.'

"When the Son of Man comes as King and all the angels with him, he will divide them into two groups, just as a shepherd separates the sheep from the goats. He will put the righteous people at his right and the others at his left. Then the King will say to the people on his right, "Come, you that are blessed by my Father! Come and possess the kingdom which has been prepared for you ever since the creation of the world. I was hungry and you fed me, thirsty and you gave me a drink; I was a stranger and you received me in your homes, naked and you clothed me; I was sick and you took care of me, in prison and you visited me."

> *The righteous will then answer him, "When, Lord, did we ever see you hungry and feed you, or thirsty and give you a drink? When did we ever see you a stranger and welcome you in our homes, or naked and clothe you? When did we ever see you sick or in prison and visit you?"*
>
> *The King will reply, "I tell you, whenever you did this for one of the least important of these brothers of mine, you did it for me!"*

When she had finished reading, she looked up at him and said, "Jesus [Hay-soos], do you know what your name is in English?"

He nodded his head and answered softly, "Jesus [Jee-zuz]."

www.ingramcontent.com/pod-product-compliance
Lightning Source LLC
Chambersburg PA
CBHW071813020426
42331CB00008B/2481